The Courage to Be Kind

Jenny Levin & Rena Rosen

Archway Publishing books may be ordered through booksellers or by contacting:

Archway Publishing
1663 Liberty Drive
Bloomington, IN 47403
www.archwaypublishing.com
1 (888) 242-5904

ISBN: 978-1-4808-3719-5 (sc)
ISBN: 978-1-4808-3717-1 (hc)
ISBN: 978-1-4808-3718-8 (e)

Print information available on the last page.

Archway Publishing rev. date: 2/6/2017

The
Courage
to Be Kind

Who Will You Be: Sam or Ellie?

"I am so proud of Rena Rosen and Jenny Levin for following their hearts and love for children of all abilities. I think this book will be a fantastic resource for parents and educators worldwide."

Katie Driscoll - Founder and President of Changing the Face of Beauty

This book is dedicated to several people who have helped support and inspire us. First, Rena's mother, Terri Mlotek, along with Rena's extended family for their love and support during this process and in life. Mary Cate Lynch and Lila Napientek for reminding Rena daily why she's doing this and for becoming her family. Jenny's parents for always being there for whatever she needs, big or small. Jenny's husband, Ryan, for his guidance and always believing in her, and Jenny's daughters, Sophie and Emma, who give her the greatest gift in the world, being their mommy.

"What's wrong with her face? Why does she look like that?"

"What happened to her legs? What is a walker?"

"Why is he so short?"

In a box of crayons, some tips are sharp and wrappers are intact. Other crayons have peeling labels and missing tips. Some are smaller than the typical crayon. Just as these crayons are still able to create something magnificent no matter their shape, color, or size, people, too, should be valued as beautiful and capable regardless of differences.

One quality we all want kids to embody is kindness for others. For parents and educators, teaching kindness and acceptance can be a tricky road.

Through the art of compassion, we are able to explicitly model, teach, and openly discuss how to navigate encounters with differences. This guidance helps kids learn to be kind to each other and accept everyone.

Conversations about physical differences can be challenging. Children are aware of surroundings and ask questions that may seem embarrassing. When children notice a distinction and announce it publicly, they are doing so with absolute honesty and a yearning to understand. This book is a resource to help guide you with the question, "Now what do I do?"

We envision a teacher or parent utilizing the book as a conversation of how one should interact with someone who looks different. To read the book, start with reading the middle text first and then comparing Ellie's interactions (top of the book) to Sam's interactions (bottom of the book). After each scenario, discuss the differences and how you can always choose to be kind.

Teaching with the art of compassion is a long road, and we hope this can be the beginning of your journey.

Rena and Jenny

It is a beautiful summer day, and the ice cream truck has just made its rounds. Everyone is enjoying the last day of summer break at Jackson Park. Ellie and Sam are building sand castles when Hannah comes over to play.

When you look at Hannah, you notice that her forehead is bigger, and her eyes stick out a little more. Hannah has Apert syndrome. Hannah's hands have four fingers. She has a hard time bending her hands because when she was born, her fingers were stuck together.

Apert Syndrome FAQ

- Apert syndrome (pronounced ay-pert) is a condition involving differences in the shape of a person's head, face, and webbing of hands and feet.

- Only 1 in 65,000–80,000 newborns are affected each year. However, several other craniofacial genetic mutations are similar in description.

- In many cases, the only symptom associated with Apert syndrome is physical. Affected people's mental capabilities are that of typical people. Sometimes people with Apert syndrome need speech therapy because of the shape of their mouths.

- Children born with Apert syndrome need to have multiple surgeries to allow for their success. Surgeries can create room in the skull where the soft spot should be, correct cleft palette, and remove webbing between fingers and toes.

- People born with Apert syndrome can lead successful and happy lives.

http://www.faces-cranio.org/pdf/APERT.pdf

Everyone is excited to pick out fun foods at the grocery store for their first day of school. Ellie really wants a cool dessert to share with friends. Sam is looking for some healthy snacks for the morning.

Max loves ice cream, video games, and watching Ohio's football team win games on TV. Max has Spina bifida. The wheelchair is one kind of support that helps Max move around to do the things he loves to do. Max uses a walker to go short distances.

Spina Bifida FAQ

- Spina bifida is a hole in the spine.

- Spina bifida develops when a baby is in the womb, and the spinal column does not close all the way. Every day, about eight babies born in the United States have Spina bifida.

- People with Spina bifida must learn to get around on their own without help by using crutches, braces, or wheelchairs.

- People born with Spina bifida can lead successful and happy lives.

http://spinabifidaassociation.org/what-is-sb/

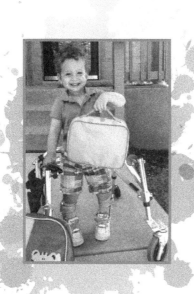

Ruthie loves school and learning. She is getting her book and folder out of her backpack. Sam and Ellie are outside the classroom, getting ready to go in.

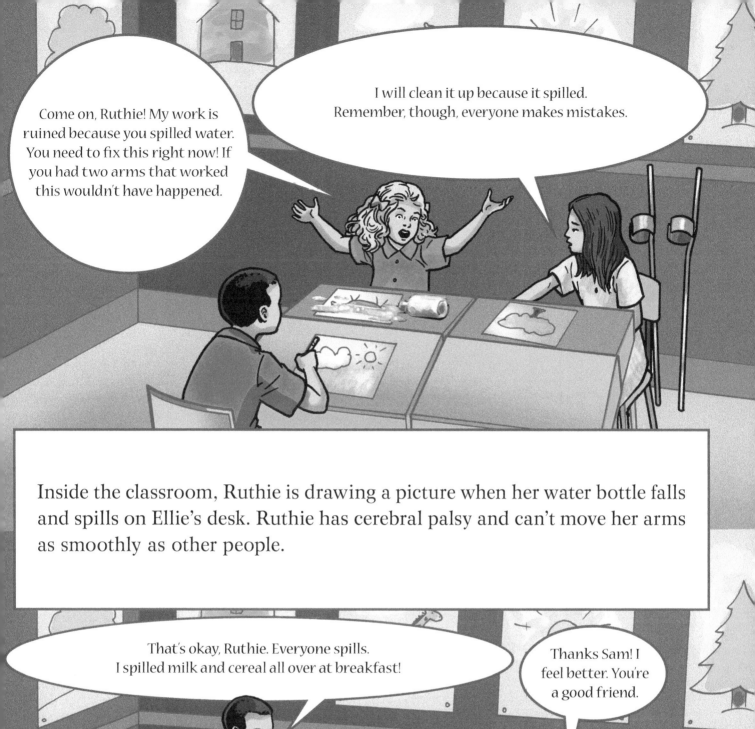

Inside the classroom, Ruthie is drawing a picture when her water bottle falls and spills on Ellie's desk. Ruthie has cerebral palsy and can't move her arms as smoothly as other people.

Cerebral Palsy FAQ

- Cerebral palsy (pronounced seh-ree-brel pawl-zee) is the loss or impairment of motor functions.

- Cerebral palsy can impact fine, gross, and oral motor skills.

- Cerebral palsy is the result of a brain injury or malformation. Affected people were most likely born with the condition, although some acquire it later.

- Every case of cerebral palsy is different. One person may need constant care, while others need very little assistance.

- People with cerebral palsy can lead successful and happy lives.

http://cerebralpalsy.org/about-cerebral-palsy/definition/

Mr. Nitzkin's class is having quiet reading time. Everyone loves it because they can sit wherever they want and enjoy their books. Ellie has gotten a book about dolphins from the library and is happily reading it when Josh starts barking.

At the beginning of every year, Josh explains to his class that he sometimes shouts and barks. He can't stop it because he has Tourette's syndrome. It is kind of like yawning or hiccupping.

Tourette Syndrome FAQ

- Tourette syndrome (TS) is a neurological condition that causes people to make sounds and movements they don't want to make and cannot control. These sounds and movements are called tics.

- There are two kinds of tics—vocal and motor.

- Some common vocal tics are sniffing, throat clearing, grunting, hooting, and shouting.

- Some motor tics are eye blinking, facial grimacing, jaw movements, head bobbing/jerking, shoulder shrugging, neck stretching, and arm jerking.

- People with Tourette syndrome can lead successful and happy lives.

http://www.tsa-usa.org/imaganw/What_is_TS_English.pdf

It's a beautiful fall day and the kids in the neighborhood are playing and running around before dinner. Bella, Sam and Ellie live on the same block. Bella is a creative, smart, and funny seven year old, and she is the height of a four year old.

Bella is a little person with an incredible imagination. She loves coming up with ideas to help her get around in a tall person's world. She wants to be an engineer when she grows up.

Dwarfism FAQ

- Little People of America defines a little person as an adult who is shorter than four feet ten inches tall.

- Such terms as "dwarf," "little person," "LP," and "person of short stature" are all acceptable, but most people would rather be referred to by their names than a label.

- Many will require surgeries or other medical interventions to address complications of bone growth and help further their movement.

- People with dwarfism can lead successful and happy lives.

http://www.lpaonline.org/faq-#Definition

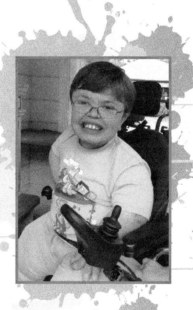

The blue and red teams are in the soccer championships. Everyone is hustling around the field, dribbling, passing, and kicking. Ava is running with the ball and about to score a goal when her wig falls off.

Ava is a healthy, athletic, soccer-loving second-grader. Ava has alopecia, which means she has no hair. Ava's body doesn't do what it needs to grow hair. This is just something that makes her unique.

Alopecia FAQ

- Alopecia (al-oh-PEE-shah) means hair loss. When a person has a medical condition called alopecia areata (ar-ee-AH-tah), the hair falls out in round patches. The hair can fall out on the scalp and elsewhere on the body.

- Alopecia areata can cause different types of hair loss. Each of these has a different name.

  - Alopecia areata (patches)
  - Alopecia totalis (all hair on the scalp)
  - Alopecia universalis (all hair on the body).

- Only 5 percent of affected people lose all of the hair on their scalps or bodies.

- People with alopecia can lead successful and happy lives.

https://www.aad.org/dermatology-a-to-z/diseases-and-treatments/a---d/alopecia-areata

The kids in art class are painting creative pictures. Paul puts shiny red paint on his picture of a wagon. Ellie asks for the paint, and some spills on Paul's arm.

Birthmarks FAQ

- Birthmarks are marks on the skin that babies are born with. Sometimes they go away; sometimes they do not.

- A port-wine stain is a stain on someone's body that looks like red wine spilled on the skin.

- Port-wine stains tend to get darker as kids get older.

- Many birthmarks cause no harm to the body.

- People with birthmarks can lead happy and fulfilling lives.

Tools for Parents and Educators

1. Most people who have conditions encourage asking questions about their differences. It is our responses to the questions that determine how children will view each difference. When children point out a difference, it is important to acknowledge what they are seeing and find a way to relate to the person so children can see similarities. Typically, it is better to ask a question that will facilitate understanding than ignore or turn away, causing embarrassment for all. Finding something in common with the person is in the art of teaching compassion. Look for similarities or common questions that you might ask any child (how old are you, what's your name, do you like …).

2. Our language helps determine how a child views a person. Instead of stating a disability label first—"the autistic kid, Jack"—it is kinder to say, "Jack, who has autism." This isn't about being politically correct but about giving everyone the chance to be a typical person with a uniqueness. When we put a label on a person, we attach a stigma to him or her.

3. Focus on what people can do rather than on what they can't do. We want to teach our children that anyone can lead meaningful and accomplished lives with hard work and a positive attitude.

4. Not every conversation or interaction will be smooth, but using open-ended questions and relating to others can help lead to choosing kindness.

For more tips and tools please visit our website at www.artocompassion.com

About the Authors

Rena is a full-time preschool teacher, a photographer, and an entrepreneur who happened to be born with a cleft lip and palate along with other craniofacial abnormalities that fall under a craniofacial syndrome. Growing up, Rena never felt different because her friends and family treated her like they would anyone else. However, she did look different, and society noticed. The stares did not bother Rena when she was younger. It was not until she was old enough to realize  and the "hello" wave had stopped working. This began to affect her self-esteem. After Rena's last surgery during college, she decided it was time to speak out and bring a higher awareness and appreciation for physical differences and the experiences that come along with those differences. Through her photography, she put together an exhibition that beautified and normalized the physical anomalies that redefine perfection. The positive response she received was the push she needed to go even further, and that is where Art of Compassion was developed. Rena took her goal of spreading kindness and awareness on the road through workshops and talks, along with friends she met on the journey, and discovered a greater community of children with craniofacial abnormalities.

Jenny graduated from The Ohio State University with a bachelor's degree in education and went to National Louis University for a master's degree in teaching. One of Jenny's biggest goals as a parent and teacher is to instill respect and kindness in students. Jenny saw an opportunity  to write a book that helps parents and teachers facilitate conversations about what to do when you encounter someone who looks different. Jenny wanted to partner with Rena to bring kindness to the forefront of education by coauthoring a book. Their excitement led to many great ideas, lots of laughter, and a whole lot of love.

References

"Definition of Cerebral Palsy—What Is CP? | CerebralPalsy.org." *CerebralPalsyorg Definition of Cerebral Palsy Comments*. N.p., n.d. Web. Aug. 6, 2015. http://cerebralpalsy.org/about-cerebral-palsy/definition/

"Excellence in Dermatology™ Excellence in Dermatologic Surgery™ Excellence in Medical Dermatology™ Excellence in Dermatopathology™." *Alopecia Areata*. N.p., n.d. Web. Aug. 6, 2015. https://www.aad.org/dermatology-a-to-z/ diseases-and-treatments/a---d/alopecia-areata

"FAQ." *FAQ*. N.p., n.d. Web. Aug. 6, 2015. http://www.lpaonline.org/faq-#Definition

"Port-Wine Stains." *KidsHealth—The Web's Most Visited Site about Children's Health*. Ed. Patrice Hyde. The Nemours Foundation, Sept. 1, 2013. Web. Aug. 6, 2015. http://kidshealth.org/parent/medical/heart/port_wine_stains.html#

"Syndrome? What Is Apert." *FACES:* (n.d.): n.p. Web. http://www.faces-cranio.org/pdf/APERT.pdf

"Tourette Syndrome." *Springer Reference* (2011): n. p. Web. http://www.tsa-usa.org/imaganw/What_is_TS_English.pdf

"What Is SB?" *Spina Bifida Association ICal*. N.p., n.d. Web. Aug. 6, 2015. http:// spinabifidaassociation.org/what-is-sb/

CPSIA information can be obtained
at www.ICGtesting.com
Printed in the USA
LVHW071135110819
627233LV00016B/207/P